Pumpkin, an orange Scottish Fold, has a transforming vision after crashing into her own reflection in the mirror....

Genevieve, a ten-year-old calico, has an out-of-body experience after one too many naps in the clothes dryer....

Pudding, a Persian suffering from chronic furballs, takes a healing journey to the Primal Purr....

Madame Blavatsky, a Russian Blue, leaves her body behind during a séance but is sent back by caring but mysterious guides....

Plus accounts of past nine lives, rubbing whiskers with feline angels, reunions in the lap of love, amazing revelations from the cat goddess Bastet—and more!

STEFANIE SAMEK is a former advertising executive who was called the "Cat Lady of Madison Avenue" for her work on the ad campaigns of Sheba and Whiskas cat foods. She is now a freelance writer and a lap to five cats.

LARRY ROSS is an illustrator who has contributed to more than 20 books, as well as the *New York Times*, *Washington Post*, *Ladies' Home Journal*, and other magazines.

Purring
in the Light

Near-Death Experiences of Cats

Stefanie Samek

Illustrations by Larry Ross

A PLUME BOOK

PLUME
Published by the Penguin Group
Penguin Books USA Inc., 375 Hudson Street,
New York, New York 10014, U.S.A.
Penguin Books Ltd, 27 Wrights Lane,
London W8 5TZ, England
Penguin Books, Australia Ltd, Ringwood,
Victoria, Australia
Penguin Books Canada Ltd, 10 Alcorn Avenue,
Toronto, Ontario, Canada M4V 3B2
Penguin Books (N.Z.) Ltd, 182–190 Wairau Road,
Auckland 10, New Zealand

Penguin Books Ltd, Registered Offices:
Harmondsworth, Middlesex, England

First published by Plume, an imprint of Dutton Signet, a division of
Penguin Books USA Inc.

First Printing, November, 1995
10 9 8 7 6 5 4 3 2 1

Copyright © Stefanie Samek, 1995
Illustrations copyright © Larry Ross, 1995
All rights reserved

Ⓟ   REGISTERED TRADEMARK—MARCA REGISTRADA

LIBRARY OF CONGRESS CATALOGING-IN-PUBLICATION DATA:
Samek, Stefanie.
    Purring in the light : near-death experiences of cats / Stefanie Samek ; illustrations
by Larry Ross.
        p.   cm.
    ISBN 0-452-27509-1
    1. Cats—Humor. 2. Near-death experiences—Humor. I. Title.
PN6231.C23S36   1995
818'.5402—dc20
                                                                    95-30204
                                                                    CIP

Printed in the United States of America
Set in Century Expanded
Designed by Leonard Telesca

Without limiting the rights under copyright reserved above, no part of this publication
may be reproduced, stored in or introduced into a retrieval system, or transmitted, in
any form, or by any means (electronic, mechanical, photocopying, recording, or other-
wise), without the prior written permission of both the copyright owner and the above
publisher of this book.

BOOKS ARE AVAILABLE AT QUANTITY DISCOUNTS WHEN USED TO PROMOTE PRODUCTS OR
SERVICES. FOR INFORMATION PLEASE WRITE TO PREMIUM MARKETING DIVISION, PENGUIN
BOOKS USA INC., 375 HUDSON STREET, NEW YORK, NEW YORK 10014.

Acknowledgments

Special thanks go to two wonderful cat lovers, Carol Abel, my agent, and Deirdre Mullane, my editor. To Larry Ross, for his hard work and witty illustrations. To my supportive family—Richard, Jennifer, Erica, my parents, and Ruth. To my teachers, Dr. Brugh Joy and David Lewine. And to my cats: Charlie, Barney, Maui, Fluffy, Sheba; as well as Catnip, Oscar, Honeybun, Buzzy, Anna & Kink, and Mad Cat Muntz—who may well be on the astral plane.

Contents

Purring
in the Light

Introduction

> Seek, and ye shall find;
> scratch, and the door shall be opened to you.
>
> Catskrit Proverb

There's not a cat alive who isn't dying to know: What happens when you go to the Great Sofa in the Sky?

When it comes to life, cats are well versed, because they have more than one. But what about death?

Life after Nine Lives?

Is there life after nine lives? And just how many lives are there? These are the questions felines have been asking since the days when they first sunbathed on the Sphinx.

What's death like? Is it like being trapped in a dark coat closet with no possible escape? Is it suddenly having nothing on your mind? Is it a long, delicious catnap, uninterrupted by hunger pangs or the need to use the litter box?

Is death a journey into another dimension, a place of end-less possibilities and infinite joy? Or is it a cold, noxious netherworld that makes your fur stand on end?

For the first time in feline history, we finally have answers to all these questions and more. From cats who've gone out and come back, we now know there's a remarkable world on the other side of that cat door.

What's Near-Death?

If you haven't died and come back, you might ask what we mean by *near*-death. Is it like being *almost* run over by a truck? Not exactly.

Feline near-death experiences have been recorded since the beginning of history. Wondrous tales of cat astral journeys are found in ancient Persian, Siamese, Burmese, and Chinese myths.

On ancient Egyptian murals we find cats crossing a river to meet the cat goddess, Bastet, at the Happy Hunting Ground. *The Burmese Book of the Dead*, written by an enlightened Burmese named Purrdmasambhava in the eighth century, de-scribes events that closely parallel the near-death experiences of cats today.

Near-death is temporarily dying, or leaving your body, and coming back to talk about it in books, on TV, at cat shows, or to any interested feline who'll listen.

It happens when cats come close to actual physical death during falls, silly mishaps, and messy accidents. It can also occur during kitten birth or nasty procedures at the vet.

It's going into a light that cuddles you in unconditional love.

It's being stroked, petted, and softly caressed by eight billion tender paws.

It's suddenly understanding your nine lives and their purpose in a transformational way.

The Near-Death Scenario

Although each scenario is unique, a typical progression of events that constitute the feline near-death experience goes like this:

A cat has a mishap. She's unconscious. Suddenly she finds herself floating over her own body.

She watches as people fuss over her. She meows to get their attention and can't. She gives up.

Although she has reason to believe she's dead, she feels good. She floats around, and listens to what everyone has to say.

She notices she can pass her paws right through her body and is completely made of light. Her *astral* fur body vibrates at a higher frequency and is especially designed for travel on the *astral plane*.

A passageway appears, some sort of tunnel, often described

as a paper bag. She floats through it, enjoying crinkling, crackling sounds, cosmic purrs of creation, and enticing scents.

She may be escorted by cat angels.

When she emerges from the tunnel, she finds herself immersed in loving light. She purrs.

A feline Light Being appears before her. It shows her more love than she ever felt in her life.

Next, she's free to visit the Celestial Warming Room or the Happy Hunting Ground, to catch up with old pals or to enjoy some astral fun and games. And if her kitty karma dictates, she drops in on the Darkside.

During a Nine Lives Review, she sees a rapid replay of her past lives and promises to reform. One of the Light Beings tells her that she's died prematurely and has to go back. She's given a mission.

The Light Beings say good-bye. She begs to stay. They promise she'll return.

She rejoins her physical body. But from that moment on, she's a different cat. Not only is she alive and still scratching—she's also dramatically transformed.

Departing Tails

Death is a dog that lies down at every door.
Swami Purrananda

What's it like to crawl out from under the final curtain? How does it feel to leave your body? And what's an astral fur body like? Does it get fleas or need to be cleaned?

Despite differences in breed type, gender, nationality, food preferences, or home life as a kitten, when we analyze the departing tails of cats, we find tremendous similarities.

Who's That Cat on the Table?

Fluffy, a severely matted silver blue Persian, was having her coat thinned, trimmed, and demated at the grooming salon. Suddenly she found herself hovering over her body. Fluffy recalls:

They'd been working on the really tough mats, the dense, tangled knots on my tummy. All at once, I found myself floating near the ceiling. I looked down and saw this limp, mangy cat lying on the table.

"Fluffy is a disgusting mess," I heard the groomer say. But when I looked at my astral fur coat, I saw silky, shining fur—in top, cat-show condition. I knew something was wrong. Then I realized that the snarled-up ball of fur on the table was me!

When I regained consciousness, I was still damp from my shampoo.

Leaving your body and suddenly finding yourself in a young, energetic vehicle with a flawless fur coat is a common occurrence.

Cats also report overhearing conversations and being unable to meow back. When Fluffy reacted to the nasty slur about her fur by hissing at the groomer, she was completely ignored.

And when cats realize they're dead, we're told, they feel elated instead of upset. As Cuddles, a three-year-old British shorthair, describes it, "It's like when you were a kitten and your mother carried you around by the scruff of your neck. You feel safe and loved."

Subjects describe an experience that's "more peaceful than an undisturbed nap in a hammock" and "more loving than a twenty-minute scratch under the chin."

Cosmic Spin Cycle

Just where does death take you? Cats report being lifted into another dimension.

A vivid description comes from a ten-year-old calico named Genevieve, who took one too many naps in the clothes dryer. Here's what she recalls:

There I am—tangled in the bras and jockey shorts— spinning like a wildcat swept up by a tornado. Then I spin right out of my body. I think I must be dead.

Hovering over the clothes dryer, I feel frisky and free. I experiment. I do back flips, free falls, and tummy floats. I fly through the clothes hamper and ironing board. On the ceiling, I discover a spider, but he doesn't seem to notice me.

Then, a thundering meow interrupts my fun. "Genevieve, you have to go back," it says.

The next thing I know, I'm lying on a pile of warm, folded underwear.

Tunnel Visions

Birth is but a catnap, and a forgetting.
William Catsworth

There you are, floating on the astral plane. Now what? Is there a scent trail to follow or someone who'll show you the way?

Although some cats describe a sensation of being "lifted into the light" and compare it to the feeling of being lovingly cuddled, most mention another kind of transition. To reach the Happy Hunting Ground, most cats say they travel through a tunnel. Tunnel visions vary, but the most common experience involves a "paper bag."

Paper Bag to the Light

Whether it's described as a grocery bag, paper sack, shopping bag, French bread bag, or cardboard box—traveling

through a dark space with paper walls is common to the near-death experience.

Cats float, fly, crawl, and stalk through this phenomenon. For some it's a fast ride; for others it's dreamy and slow. Some cats say they have the whole bag to themselves. Others share the experience.

Of course, when there's a cataclysm, the tunnel gets more traffic. But even bumper-to-bumper, cats float along in a state of bliss.

Raggedy Ann, a mitted Ragdoll, gives us a typical account:

One minute I was munching on the TV cord, the next—complete darkness! I knew it was more than a power failure. I noticed that my white paws had this strange, iridescent glow.

Suddenly, I found myself floating along in this enormous, dark place—like a vast paper bag. The walls were brown, wrinkly, crinkly, crumpled paper. Way off in the distance, I could see that the far end of the bag was torn open. Simmering white light was pouring in. Other cats floated by me. Everyone was very friendly. As we gently ricocheted off the walls of the bag, a crinkling paper cantata accompanied us. I never felt more peaceful or content.

Chanel, the chocolate point Siamese of a shopaholic, had a near-death experience when a clothes rack collapsed, burying her under a mountain of designer outfits. She recalls:

I knew I was dead because that irritating Chanel cat collar was no longer choking me around the neck.

I found myself floating in a vast shopping bag. I drifted along, feeling like some objet d'art that was being carried home to be treasured.

Then, all at once some unseen force picked up the bag and turned it upside down. Suddenly, I spilled back into my body. As I crawled out from under a navy knit Valentino dress and a pink St. Laurent suit, I knew I was home.

A Stairway of Shoeboxes

When Zoe, a tiny tortoiseshell Persian, inhaled a misdirected spritz of Maxi Megahold hair spray, she skipped the tunnel and took the stairs. She describes:

"So this is death," I thought, finding myself curled up in a size-five shoebox and experiencing a peace beyond all purrs.

After a delicious snooze, I woke up and looked around. I couldn't believe my sleepy eyes. I realized that my shoebox was part of a towering stairway of shoeboxes that led straight to the stars.

I climbed the shoebox stairway, joyously leaping from box to box. It was leading higher and higher. Straight up

to a lofty carpeted perch that was bathed in a magnificent, radiant white light. Up, up, up, I scooted.

But instead of reaching the Promised Perch, I regained consciousness on a prickly pile of hair rollers.

I Followed the Silver String

The tunnel experience may be solitary or social. Some cats are drawn into the tunnel by curiosity. Some say they're escorted through the tunnel by Light Beings, guardian angels, or old pals.

When a playful Tonkinese named Bamboo crashed into a skateboard and left his body, he was led into the tunnel by a string.

First, I'm standing there in the dark. Then I spot this luminous, totally irresistible piece of silver string that seems to be dangling out of nowhere.

I bat at the string. It gives off zillions of dazzling, glittering sparks. Like it's alive, with a mind all of its own.

I begin to chase the string. It spins and whirls and

whips around like a luminescent lariat. For miles and miles, I chase the string through a foil tunnel.

I dance into a pool of blinding white light.

Tunneling under the Celestial Sheets

Pumpkin, an orange Scottish Fold who suffered a concussion after crashing into her own reflection in the mirror, describes another kind of tunnel:

I found myself burrowing through a long, dark space— that reminded me of bed covers. I was enveloped by acres and acres of soft cotton and cushy down comforting. There were delicious folds to hide in, as well as enticing stray threads and loose hems to yank.

At one end, where the covers were loose, I could see an otherworldly light. I sensed something wonderful was out there.

Tunnel visions may vary, but cats agree on one thing. No earth journey down a dark hole can match its rewards.

Sound Bites from Beyond

Perk up your ears; someone's trying to show you the way.

Upurranasheds

Like cat life, cat afterlife has its own colorful palette of sounds. Cats describe complex sound tapestries that aren't just heard but are intensely felt.

These ear-tweaking noises run the gamut—from earthly to otherworldly. Beautiful to strange. Cats also report hearing long, low rumbles and a pulsating, purring vibration that's known as the *Primal Purr*.

But the Meows of the Spheres aren't always music to feline ears.

Heavenly Snaps, Crackles, and Pops

We're told that each experience comes with a special sound track. For example, the paper-bag tunnel has a sound system

so fantastic that, when cats come back, they're often de-pressed. Life suddenly sounds dull. As though somebody turned down the volume and filtered out the fun.

Clovis, a young tabby tiger who had a bad reaction to a rug shampoo, wistfully recalls her near-death trip:

It began with a symphony of small, enticing crackles, like millions of pieces of cellophane being crumpled. I could hardly stand the excitement!

Next came a chorus of snaps, crackles, and pops. They thundered right through me, reverberating off every whisker. I noticed my astral fur coat was standing on end.

I didn't think it could get any better, but it did. I was surrounded by the sounds of an enormous, wrinkled paper bag being folded and unfolded. Again and again and again. My astral ears were on fire. My senses were alive. I could literally hear through my fur.

The Primal Purr

According to ancient Catskrit manuscripts, the universe began with a sound. And the sound was *purrrrr*.

In the beginning there was only the purr. Some say this Purr of Creation was the sound responsible for all life.

During near-death, most cats say they hear the Primal Purr.

It's a purr with amazing powers. It's been known to heal, transform, enlighten, and bring love.

An example of its power comes from Pudding, an orange mixed-breed longhair with a history of chronic furballs.

One near-fatal furball carried her on a healing journey:

Gagging on the furball, I went unconscious, and suddenly left my body. Then I found myself floating in this great dark Void.

But it wasn't a silent Void. It purred. Not an ordinary purr, like yours or mine, but a thunderous purr. A magnificent, roaring rumble that hummed, droned, and buzzed.

I not only heard the purr—I *was* the purr. It vibrated right through my whiskers and claws.

Not even the loud, reassuring purrs of ten million contented mother cats—purring with adoration for their kittens—compared with this purr in its beauty or ability to express absolute, unconditional love.

Since her experience, Pudding has never choked on another furball. She attributes it to the healing powers of the Primal Purr.

Heavenly Scents

The nose knows what the whiskers can only guess.
                                          Ancient Abyssinian affurism

Feline near-death experiences tell us how the afterlife looks, feels, and sounds. They also tell us how it smells. There's a wondrous world that's seen through the nose.

Smells. Glorious smells. Scent marks. Scent trails. Scent paths. Whiffs. Sniffs. Snootsful. Every odor that ever was. In the afterlife, cats are free to sniff them all.

A Feast for My Senses

Here's how Tiny, a nineteen-pound gray tiger cat, described a brief near-death experience he had during a transatlantic flight. He says that while he was out of his body, he enjoyed some of the best smells in his life:

Suddenly, I found myself at the bottom of a giant food bowl. The bowl was being filled with the smells of all my favorite foods.

First, it smelled as if tuna were being spooned over my entire body. Then I was smothered in the delicious, fishy scents of Supreme Seafood Feast.

Wonderful sounds heightened the ecstasy—the whir of an electric can opener, the rip of a pop-up lid, and a thunderous rumbling of kibbles. Crashing scent waves of shrimp, mackerel, cod, and sole enveloped me. I devoured the smells.

Finally, I gobbled up the fragrances of an entire Thanksgiving dinner.

Everyone Smells Friendly

The smells of Purradise aren't limited to food. When Spot, a three-year-old spotted shorthair, choked on her catnip mouse, she found herself surrounded by friendly scents:

I knew I wasn't alone. I could smell animals and people everywhere. They were floating all around me: cats, dogs, mice, chipmunks, birds, squirrels. Lots of species I'd never smelled before.

But the big difference was that they all smelled

friendly. I didn't catch a whiff of anything unpleasant. Their sweet scents said they were feeling only joy.

A Trip to the Park

Jasmine, a sensitive Balinese, has spent her entire life in a studio apartment overlooking Central Park. When she left her body during a routine visit to the vet, she says she dropped in on the park.

As Dr. Hanes was giving me a shot, I zipped up to the corner of the examining room and sailed straight out through the ceiling.

I wafted over Central Park and finally touched down on the Great Lawn. It smelled the way I always imagined it would. Spring smells. Pigeon droppings. Dog droppings. People. Flowers. Grass. Earthworms. Birds. New York air.

I was intoxicated by it. I rolled in the grass, inhaling huge snootsful of the scents. Then—whoosh! I felt myself slip back into my body through the space between my ears. Once again, it smelled like the vet's.

I opened my eyes to see Dr. Hanes checking my teeth for tartar.

Sexy Scents

With a sly twinkle in his yellow eyes, Roland, a stocky brown tabby and notorious feline-izer, recalls a near-death experience he had when an ironing board collapsed on him.

I smelled the scent of every cat I ever loved. Their divine fragrances filled the air. I was in sensory heaven.

There was Bambi's fur. Comet's belly. Angel's cheeks. Babette's neck. Bitsie's breath. Whiffenpoof's whiskers.

I smelled the pink pads on Cuddle's paws. Jinx. Sweetie Pie. Isis. Tinkerbell's tail. Miss Priss. Tara. Mai Tai. Ernestine's ears. BJ's back. Paloma's puss. Tuxedo's front. Sapphire's back. Mai Tai's mitts. Muffy. Binky. Chat Noir's chin. Catapoof's ruff. And Dawn.

Every cat we spoke with concurred: Nosing around on the Other Side is one of near-death's greatest delights.

Lapping Up
the Light

To see in the dark, look with the eye that sees the true light.

Catskrit Proverb

Nearly every near-death account contains a mention of the light. Cats say they're cuddled, hugged, petted, kissed, stroked, warmed, licked, fluffed, brushed, healed, and transformed by it.

They drink it in and lap it up. They bathe in it. This light, cats say, is the high point of near-death. Yet in describing it, meows fail them.

They tell us the light is blazing white. Or yellow-white. Or blue-white. Or shimmering yellow-gold. And it's the highest wattage that ever was, blazing brighter than a million suns on a hot summer day.

Yet they say that the light never hurts your eyes. It's gentle and loving; it doesn't make you squint the way you do when you wake up from a catnap in the blinding sun.

Cats who've been brushed by the light return with more than just a shinier coat. The light, they say, is made of pure love. Besides warming your fur, enriching your purr, and putting joy in your heart, the light also has the power to transform you.

A Net of Lights

Chester, a portly fifteen-year-old British shorthair, remembers "falling into the light" during his experience of near-death:

The sparrow was too scrumptious to pass up. Like a fool, I followed her up the tree. But I was no kitten. All of a sudden—snap!

Suddenly, I was outside my body, watching myself hurtle through the air: legs flailing, tail flying, falling straight down.

I fell and fell, straight into a luminous net made of blazing white lights. It caught me, soft as a cloud, and gently set me down.

When I came to at the base of the tree, I could still sense the net of lights all around me. I know it saved my life.

Zillion-Watt Lamp

With some cats, the light is described as the ultimate heat source. When Vanna, a three-year-old yellow tabby, fell into an icy stream on a dark, rainy day, she left her body through the space between her ears. When she got to the Other Side, she was no longer cold.

I found myself basking under this colossal heat lamp, with a zillion-watt bulb. I lay directly under it. The light blazed down on my fur. I was ecstatic. Besides making me warm, it made me feel loved all over.

Then the lamp spoke to me. It said, "The light's going off. You're going back."

And there I was—on the cold, hard shore.

The Light Took Out the "Ouch"

Tinkerbell, a tiny, silver shorthair, saw the light after a neighbor's Yorkie gave her a nasty nip. She describes the light's miraculous healing power:

I passed out and floated up. Prince Edward still had me by the leg, but I didn't feel a thing.

A loving light surrounded me. It felt hot and healing.

When I came to, Prince Edward had stopped biting. He just stood there staring at me, with his tongue hanging out, looking dazed.

I saw light all around my fur. He could see it too. Where he'd nipped, the bite mark had vanished along with the pain. The light took away the "ouch."

Whiskered Light Beings

Since so many cats describe a Being of Light who resembles the King of the Beasts, we've included one example.

Jellybean, a young calico, left her body during a raging snowstorm. She remembers:

The sky was a shower of shimmering diamonds. Then He appeared. An enormous luminous lion made of liquid golden light.

The ground shook as he walked. His golden eyes twinkled and blazed. Shooting stars flew from his mane. Dazzling sparks danced off his paws. When his whiskers twitched, they sent out long, radiant beams of light.

His glittering golden eyes looked into mine with a look that said he'd known me from the beginning of time.

"Your person's lap would be empty without you. You have to go back," he roared lovingly.

With that, I awoke in the folds of her denim skirt. We were by a fire, and she was dusting the last flakes of snow from my fur.

Cat Angels

You're always touching noses with your angels.
Swami Purrananda

Cat angels have been watching over felines since the first primordial meow.

Protecting cats is their business. Dropping down to give directions is their basic task. They show up for arrivals and departures. And, whenever they're needed, in between. Cat angels are just as much a fact of life as they are a fact of death.

We've learned there's a whole hierarchy of winged whiskered beings. Seven separate categories. Each with its own special mission.

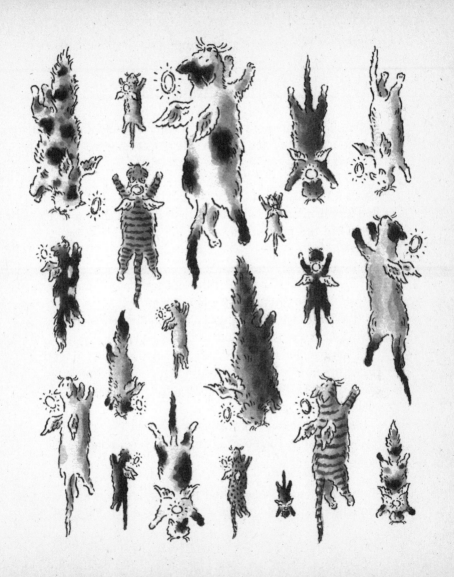

Guardian Angel Cats

Bingo is an orange striped tabby whose near-fatal fall carried him to new spiritual heights. He says he met his guardian angel, and it changed the course of his life.

I was a reckless kinda cat who lived on the edge. Like I had fifteen or twenty lives. So when I fell off the roof and landed in the paws of my guardian angel, I was pretty amazed.

"So I'm dead?" I asked.

"Yes, you are," he said. "But not for long. Before you return, I want to show you a few things."

We floated around together for a while. He said he'd always help me. If I needed him, he'd be there.

Then we floated over my dead body. I was surprised to see my family in tears. I could actually feel their emotions. For the first time, I understood how much they really cared.

With that thought, I was back in my body. I twitched my whiskers and rubbed against the warm hand on my head.

Every cat has its own guardian angel. Some have two. Some, who need more guarding, may even have a few. Many

cats have told us that near-death was the first time they'd actually touched noses with their guardian angels.

For nine lives, they're on your case. They help you work out your kitty karma. And avoid ferocious dogs.

Angel Escort Service

Although the Other Side offers a panoply of exotic destinations, we've been told you won't get lost. A second category of cat angels provides an Escort Service. The angels in this band of sweet-faced apricot Persians are masters of the universe. With silky wings flapping, they gladly act as guides.

An aristocratic Cornish Rex named Lord Woolsy met his first Persian Angel Escort after a yachting accident. As he tells it:

I'm dead, you see, and there they are, floating toward me—two magnificent apricot Persian angels.

They take my paws in their paws, lift me up, and ask me where I want to go.

"What are the choices?" I ask. They say I can visit earth, cruise around heaven, play in the Happy Hunting Ground, catch up with chums who've passed on, review my past lives, or curl up in the Celestial Warming Room. I imagine myself luxuriating on an embroidered velvet pillow, and, in a whisker's twitch, that's where I am.

Cat Cupids

"Before my near-death experience," says Hector, a darkly handsome twelve-year-old Havana with brooding green eyes, "I always wondered why love gave me so much pain."

When a virus moved into Hector's body, he moved out and met our third category of angels on the astral plane. The cats who play Cupid. Those softly purring celestial experts on romance and sex. He tells us:

Beautiful felines have always been my downfall. A pair of angelic felines showed me why. To find the answer, we flew back to one of my previous lives.

I discovered that, in that life, I had been a magnificent female feline and a cunning, seductive temptress. This calculating Egyptian Mau entertained herself by telling poor, heartsick toms to go jump in the Nile. My past actions made me hiss!

The Cat Cupids told me my current kitty karma is to chase after cats I can't catch. I didn't like the answer, but it made perfect karmic sense. I also learned that in heaven, you don't mess with the cat angels. When I tried to make a move on the glossy Angora with huge blue eyes, I landed back in my body.

That gorgeous flying fluffball tossed me right off the astral plane!

Hector says he's learned from this experience. Instead of being such a tail chaser, he's chosen to lead a more spiritual life.

When his karmic dues are paid, Hector says he'll be ready to find his love match. He hopes some silky-pawed beauty will be his final catch.

The Cat Cupids do more than arrange feline love matches. We're told they're also responsible for the Love Bonds between cats and their kittens, cats and their humans, and cats and other creatures.

These days, a big part of their work is helping strays and shelter cats and kittens find a little love that lasts.

Guardians of the Snooze

Because cats spend so much time napping, special cat angels are designated as guardians of sleep. They oversee catnaps, long delicious snoozes, and the world of dreams.

We're told that when a cat leaves its body during a dream, these angels rush in. If a cat has a nightmare, they may intercede.

They also make sure that sleeping cats who are on the astral prowl stay safely connected to their bodies by their astral silver cord. If the cord gets tangled up, they fly in to

straighten it out. Gremlin, a small gray-and-white tiger cat, first encountered a Guardian of the Snooze during a dream of near-death.

My human left the oven open. I crawl in and immediately fall asleep next to an unbaked blueberry pie.

The next thing I know, I'm having a dream. In the dream, I see her close the oven. She's about to turn it on. Then the scene fades. Next, I see a gossamer angel with sea-green eyes. This angel floats up to me and starts flipping her tail. "Wake up," she says. "You're not supposed to die!"

So I wake up and hop out of the oven. My human sees me, and this time she's the one who almost dies.

Guardians of the Snooze wake up sleeping cats who are in danger and arouse catnapping cats when it's time to eat, play, or make love.

These cat angels are also in charge of creature comforts. Cats call on Guardians of the Snooze when there are territorial disputes over soft spots.

We've heard that you don't need a near-death experience to see Guardians. Just be more wide awake when you dream.

A Meowing Muse

Dante is a black-and-white shorthair who lives with a painter in Rome. One day, a tainted plate of sardines flung him onto death's doorstep.

During Dante's slow recovery, his artist-provider was unable to paint. As Dante drifted in and out of his body, a fifth

category of cat angel appeared by his side. This purring appurition said that she was his muse and that all artists' cats have
their own special angels. These angelic, meowing messengers
channel creative inspiration to artists' cats. Dante explains:

> I couldn't believe my eyes. Descending on a cloud, mew-
> ing a mystical aria, this *angelina* appears. So *bella*, this

stardusted *gattina,* with azure-blue eyes and fluffy wings. She carried a tiny paintbrush in one paw and a tiny fish-bone harp in the other.

She told me I must go on living because my artist-provider couldn't paint without me.

She said she'd always float down when I needed inspiration. Then she kissed me *ciao* and good-bye.

Dante says that since his near-death experience, his artist-provider has gone on to become a world-famous painter of cats and has even been compared to Leonardo da Vinci.

With a twinkle coming into his yellow eyes, he confesses, "We get lots of celestial assistance. When we need a good idea, I meow and she's there."

Angels of the Night

We're told that a sixth category of cat angels rules over the night, the occult, all things paranormal, mysterious, magical, and unseen.

They also help witches find familiars, assist at séances, predict earthquakes, help with astral projections and appuritions, and have their paws especially full on Halloween. Here's an example.

Madame Blavatsky is a Russian Blue who works with one of the top fortune-tellers in Hollywood. She admits to being her person's confidante, familiar, channel, lucky charm, and bed warmer.

After a month of nonstop readings right before the Academy Awards, Madame Blavatsky felt as though she might be getting a bug.

During a Saturday-night séance, she felt fuzzy-headed and passed out right in the middle of the circle. She remembers:

> All at once I found myself surrounded by three angels. Black goddesses of the night. They carried me through the starry skies, purring at me softly, stroking my head with their soft, loving paws.

While Madame Blavatsky was on the Other Side, the Angels of the Night made themselves known at the séance. Here's what happened while she was gone:

> After I flopped over and passed out, I was told three black cat angels appeared and hovered over the séance table! The clients were just flabbergasted. They figured we'd conjured the whole thing up.
>
> Telepathically, the cat angels told my person to rush me to the vet. I had a life-threatening infection. But thanks to them, I was saved.
>
> Our clients keep asking when those furry appuritions will drop by.

Celestial Police

Discovering there's a pussycat posse of cat angel police has given cats a new sense of security.

"I enjoy longer catnaps, knowing there's someone looking down on me," says one indolent Manx. "If some dog tries to mess with me, I ask one of them cat angel *coppers* to step in," a British shorthair adds.

A heartwarming story of the Celestial Police's rescue service was given to us by Periwinkle, a young and rambunctious blue point Tonkinese.

One spring day, Periwinkle and her sister Bluebell were

playing in the woods. Periwinkle dashed off in pursuit of an orange butterfly and flipped off a dead log into a ditch.

She remembers meowing for help from the spot where she lay, and then passing out of her body.

I saw a band of cat angels zooming in my direction. Their purrs sounded like Harley-Davidsons. They were stocky orange toms in golden helmets. Flying in formation, they roared in and picked me up.

"Not to worry, kitty," one cat said. "You're a little banged up, but you're not dead. Let's get your sister. She'll help you out."

With that, we sped to the spot in the woods where my sister was sunning herself on a rock. One of the police meowed something in her ear. The next second she was off, racing toward my injured body faster than a speeding puma.

With that, I woke up. My sister's rough tongue was washing my face.

Although we hear many stories of rescue and love, we're told these soft-pawed cosmic law enforcers also help direct astral traffic, act as crossing-over guards at cat reincarnations, and safeguard the earth from an onslaught of fleas.

No matter which of the seven categories of cat angels is officiating, cats are always protected and surrounded by love.

The Celestial Warming Room

Three Precious Blessings:
a warm fur coat, an inner fire, a radiant heart.
Dharmapurrdmeow

For every shivering mouser with frozen whiskers and icy paws; for every cat left out in the cold by blanket-stealing people; for every trembling Devon Rex or hairless Sphinx, the afterlife holds a warm reward.

It's most commonly known as the Celestial Warming Room. We've also heard it called the Hot House, Bake Shop, Torrid Zone, Divine Inferno, and Feline Furnace.

The Celestial Warming Room is a place where cats are in their favorite element: heat. In this heavenly halfway house, heat-seeking felines find all the warmth they've been searching for, curl up, and get a little rest.

Hot Spots

Even though Stanley inherited the thick fur coat of his Maine Coon mother and the sturdy constitution of his tabby father, he says he's always felt chilly. His job in a meat-packing plant didn't help.

"The more I yowled about the cold, the colder I'd be," he says.

One day, Stanley got trapped in the refrigeration room with the frozen turkeys. While he almost froze to death, he visited the Celestial Warming Room. He recalls:

After a trip down a tunnel, I came to a desert of kitty litter, where it was a scorcher of a summer day. Heat shimmered off the hot, white sand. I padded along for a few yards, and the litter began to part. I saw a round, domed room and floated in.

The room was alive with cats warming their bodies under the hot desert sun. Cats were sprawled out on pillows, poufs, under cat cozies, and on hot cushions. Toasting cats were wall-to-wall.

I floated to a plump, cream, satin pillow and immediately sank in. The softness and heat reminded me of my mother's underbelly.

Despite the large feline turnout, no one was territorial. Sharing our body heat only added to our bliss. I could have stayed there forever.

Then, suddenly I heard a click and felt the cold as my boss opened the refrigeration room door.

The Divine Inferno

When cats find themselves in a hot, fiery place it doesn't mean they've died and gone to hell.

Amber, a red Abyssinian, made the mistake of walking into the line of fire while her family members were spraying themselves with Jungle Barrier insect spray.

This resulted in a short trip to a place she refers to as the Divine Inferno.

I'm in a throbbing red room. The walls pulsate with neon waves of heat. We curl up on crushed-velvet crimson sofas. Thermal lamps blaze down from the ceiling. We're on fire. Waves of heat dance off our fur. We roll around in ecstasy.

In the center of the circle of sofas there's an enormous warming pit with a massive, roaring fire. Some cats lie close to it, listening to the crackles and studying the sparks. Reflections of the flames flicker in their eyes. As the unrelenting warmth spreads over our bodies, our purrs become a roar. The temperature rises.

Then, all at once, I feel a cold sensation. Like metal against my fur. I open my eyes. I've left the Divine Inferno. I see I'm at the vet.

Experiences like these give cats hope. They tell us that, no matter how cold-blooded life may seem, there's heat as well as light at the end of the tunnel.

Rendezvous with a Cat Goddess

Honor the goddess who purrs within.
Egyptian Book of the Mau

For more than two thousand years in ancient Egypt, cats worshiped at the paws of Bastet, the cat goddess of love, sex, fertility, the night, and the moon.

To serve in her temple was a sacred honor. To be mummified in her name not only helped you cross over. It also guaranteed you a good seat on the astral plane.

Catroglyphic scratchings on Egyptian tomb walls show us that the near-death experiences cats were having before the introduction of canned tuna aren't much different from the ones today.

Although a host of meowing messiahs, silken-pawed saints, and whiskered idols from books, movies, television, and cartoons have padded through the feline pantheon of deities since Bastet, she's still the Queen of Queens.

Kali's Story

The Cat Cult of Bastet not only transcends time; it also cuts across all cultural barriers.

Kali is a three-year-old brown shorthair from India. In her family, there was no cat goddess. Only an elephant god named Ganesha.

"We had a statue of Ganesha in our garden. I'd rub up against his trunk and lay my offerings at his feet," she says.

But when a near-fatal snake bite spun Kali into the Realm of the Gods, she didn't meet an elephant. She met a cat. Kali recalls:

I'm crawling through an enormous, dark basket. Light pours in through open reeds at one end. As I get closer, I see a figure in the light.

It is feline. She is regal. She is serene. There is a loving expression on her face. She is the most beautiful creature I've ever seen. A halo of golden white light dances off her large, noble ears. She holds a musical instrument in one paw. She shakes it. The sound is healing. There's a litter of kittens at her feet, and I stop to nuzzle them.

I know who she is. There's no mistaking her. She is the Goddess. The Supreme Light Being. She is Bastet.

Memories of meeting the cat goddess never left Kali's mind. And Bastet, it turns out, was never far away. One day while she was chasing a fly across a pile of books, Kali's paw suddenly stopped on a volume about ancient Egypt. She remembers:

> A strong sense of her presence came over me. I felt her guide my paw to open the book and flip to a particular page. And there it was—a sculptured likeness of Bastet, just as I remembered her. Now I know I'm never alone.

A Message from Bastet

No cat can help wondering: After thousands of years of cat worship, what happened? Why did it end?

Was Bastet catnapping on the job? Were the temple cats out of their bodies when the human deities arrived on the scene and grabbed control?

Several cats who've met Bastet on the Other Side have been shown the meaning of everything that's ever happened to cats since the beginning of time.

One of the most detailed messages was given to a sultry Sphinx named Riddle, when she had a near-death experience from choking on a chicken bone.

"Meeting Bastet has helped me find my purpose. It changed my life," Riddle says. Here's what she recalls:

Bastet and I had a telepathic conversation. I understood that she is the Cat Goddess of all Creation. Her mission is to show the world how to express its feline nature: to be gentle, loving, nurturing, sensitive, self-sufficient, intuitive, instinctive, tender, graceful, and One With All. Like a cat.

When I wanted to know why cats were no longer worshiped as gods, she told me. She said that in ancient Egypt, cats got a little power-hungry and turned their humans into servants. That's when the trouble began.

She also said that many cats made the mistake of flaunting their intelligence and supernatural power. When humans began to fear they were losing control, they put their own gods in charge.

Bastet said, "Look in the museums. My statues tell the story. In the beginning I was all feline. Then they pierced my ear. A necklace came next. Then a rattle. When they gave me the body of a woman and the head of a cat, I knew it was the end."

Bastet also said that the current passion for cats shows a positive shift in world consciousness. She told me my mission was to go back and help everyone get in touch with their inner feline.

Riddle's meeting with Bastet gave her more than answers. It gave her a purpose. Currently, she leads Inner Cat Seminars, lobbies for feline rights, and is raising funds to build a temple to Bastet in New York's Catskill Mountains. The Cult of the Cat may soon be back.

The Happy Hunting Ground

Death is what you make of it.
The Burmese Book of the Dead

For most cats, the Happy Hunting Ground is the real Promised Land. They say it's a place where you can hunt anything that comes to mind. And catch it.

No prey is too vicious, too clever, too fast, too slow, too big, or too small to pursue. And because it's heaven, no one gets hurt in the end.

For every mouser who ever waited by an empty mouse hole; for every chipmunk chaser left in the lurch; for every tree-climbing birder who fell off a branch, the Happy Hunting Ground is to die for.

If Cats Could Fly

Cats tell us that not even the finest flying dreams can compare with the near-death experience of flight.

In the Happy Hunting Ground, cats use this ability to chase after birds. A down-to-earth beige shorthair called Phoebe fondly recalls her flight:

> In the high desert, where I live, I see lots of hawks and eagles. I always wanted to fly like them.
>
> While I was in the Happy Hunting Ground, I created an enormous eagle by using my imagination. Then I flew after it, flying over mountains, valleys, rivers—swooping and soaring, I purred the whole way.

Miss Ritz Gets Her Revenge

For one cat, the Happy Hunting Ground proved itself to be a land of opportunity where she was able to work out real-life frustrations through near-death revenge.

The story comes to us from Miss Ritz, a svelte lilac point Siamese living on the ground floor of a high-rise. She says that every morning a dog walker, with a large brace of dogs, would pass by her window. The dogs never missed a chance to bark lewd remarks.

Trapped behind glass, she had little recourse. She'd hiss, snarl, or simply look the other way.

But when she left her body after eating three-day-old cod canapés, Miss Ritz was finally able to live out her canine fantasy. As she tells it:

In the Happy Hunting Ground, I found I could use my imagination to make things appear. I practiced by creating a pretend mouse and chasing it until I got bored. Then I thought up a chipmunk and trailed him through the glowing green grass.

Suddenly, those low-life hounds came to mind. And there they were! The poodle, corgi, Rottweiler, Labrador, Russian wolfhound, whippet, and basset hound. They just stood there, looking at me, waiting for some kind of command.

I made them do silly dog tricks. I had them perform flips and twirls, jump through hoops, shake paws with one another, retrieve things I threw, and stand on their heads. My whiskers ached from laughing.

Now that I'm back in my body, I still see the dogs every day, but I don't see them in the same way. When they pass by my window, I have a new trick of my own. I send them love.

A Fish Story

Nanook is a Norwegian Forest cat who lives in the Canadian Rockies. He had a near-death experience as a result of tumbling off a cliff. It included an out-of-this-world fishing trip.

I knew I wasn't dreaming, because everything was so real. Nature was more "heavenly" than it is in life. The light was brighter. The colors were more vivid. The smells were more intense.

I was by a salmon stream. Every drop of water was alive. The salmon were huge. They glittered in the sun. They fluttered and flip-flopped. As soon as I thought about catching one, a small fish jumped right into my paws. I threw it back and tried again.

This time, a two-foot salmon jumped into my paws. I threw it back and tried again. I thought of a six-foot salmon—and there it was. Although the fish was huge, keeping my grip on it was easy! I was the king of fisher-cats, and this was my Happy Fishing Ground!

Fun House

One cat we spoke with is a grand champion Ocecat named Dot. When Dot picked up an exotic virus, his life in the limelight almost came to an end.

Although Dot made a speedy recovery, he says he was in no rush to return. His Happy Hunting Ground adventure included a visit to a cat amusement park:

There was Kitty Golf, where I batted around dozens of bouncing balls.

There were huge trees to climb, with moving limbs that gently put you back down on the ground.

The Fun House had a mirror room, where I chased my own reflection. Another room had enormous floating feathers.

A Cat Tease Ride took me through a dark passage, where ropes, wires, peacock feathers, and string sprang out from every direction.

I even sailed down a giant slide that tossed me into a room filled with wild, whirling autumn leaves.

If life is school, then death must be recess. The Happy Hunting Ground is where felines pause to play.

Reunions in the Lap of Love

You never have to meow "sayonara."
Japanese Bobtail Proverb

None of us likes to let go of something we love, whether it's a good friend or a well-worn spot on the sofa. However, attachment is the root of feline suffering. It's like having your claws stuck in the rug.

There's the lap you've loved for the past ten years. The person who shares your pillow. The dog you trained to roll you the ball. The tom who joins you for afternoon hunts. How do you ever let go?

Accounts from cats who've seen ahead have given us a new perspective. We've learned that good-byes aren't really for good. You don't just turn your tail and walk away: *Forever* means there's more to come.

On the Other Side, we meet again. At intimate love-fests and extended family reunions, cats catch up with beloved people, littermates, and treasured pet pals.

You can sniff out new friends or snuggle up with old ones. Brush tails with famous names from history, the arts, politics, cat shows, and the world of the hunt. In this lap-hopper's heaven, you even get to meet celebrities you only read about in *Fur People* magazine.

The Family Tree

Muffin is a two-year-old tortoiseshell who was orphaned at an early age. During near-death, she got to touch noses with some of her ancestors.

It began and ended with a tree. Muffin was climbing a large maple, when a branch snapped and flung her to the ground. Muffin recalls:

My guardian angel took me by the paw and led me to a magnificent flowering cherry tree. The pale pink petals seemed to be alive with energy. Instead of bark, the wide branches of the tree were covered in soft, green moss.

Suddenly I heard it. The whole tree purred. Then I saw why! Cats! Cats were perched on every branch of the tree.

My guardian angel told me each one was a relative. On the bottom branch, I met my mother. She was over-joyed to see me. Lovingly, we cleaned each other's coats

and rubbed heads. Then she introduced me to the rest of the family as we climbed our tree.

There were orange, blue-cream, and lavender-cream torties; tabby torties and patchwork torties; black-and-white shorthairs, calicos, solid blacks, whites, grays, even an Abyssinian and a Siamese!

My mother told me I still had work to do on earth. I meowed that I didn't want to leave, but she said there were still empty branches to fill on our tree.

Muffin returned to raise six beautiful litters of kittens. She reminded each kitten that it was special—and never forgot her family tree.

Same Old Bone

Murphy, a massive silver tabby who's getting on in years, has seen the passing of many animal acquaintances. But during several near-death experiences, he's been able to catch up with them.

After a recent collision with a swinging door, Murphy ran into a deceased canine friend named Mr. Lucky. He recalls:

There he was, coming through the light, gleefully wagging his stupid tail—my old canine chum and longtime companion, a golden retriever named Mr. Lucky.

We had kept company in many lives. In most of them, he smelled doggie and had fleas. But up here, Mr. Lucky smelled good.

"Hey, Mr. Lucky," I said. "You still up here? What's wrong? Doesn't anybody on earth want a flea-ridden, mindless mutt?"

"Good to see you, you sleazy ball of fluff," he barked. "I've missed your dumb feline face!"

Then he went back to gnawing on the same bone he'd been chewing for at least ten lives.

Grandma Was a Snow Leopard

Most cats love to imagine that in some past life they were a lion, a tiger, a jaguar, a leopard, a panther, or a puma.

It's one thing to fantasize but quite another to find out it's true. Even as a tiny orange kitten, Tiger felt his name matched his soul's true identity. Watching *The Lion King* sent chills through his fur.

"Just like a little tiger," his family would say, watching the wild way he'd stalk, pounce, and chase after anything that so much as fluttered. Unfortunately, this only fueled his vanity. But one day someone proved he was no King of the Beasts. On the front lawn, Tiger fell prey to his prey. He recalls:

I looked down and saw myself lying motionless, in the clutches of a small, biting beast. Then I found myself floating up—just as the chipmunk was scampering away.

Out of the light, two brilliant cat's eyes appeared, ice blue and glowing with love. It was my grandmother from a former life. A majestic snow leopard. She nuzzled me as if I were her kitten and licked my fur. We spoke without uttering a single meow, but so much love was shared and understood.

We floated to a high mountaintop, like those in Tibet, where we played, slept, and stretched in the bright blue air.

She told me not to be so vain, pointing out that even beautiful snow leopards are beginning to vanish from the earth. She said we're all endangered species.

Then she gave me some good hunting tips and nuzzled me good-bye.

Cleopatra's Cat

The feline near-death experience has been known to open tightly sealed and hidden doors to past, and even future, lives. It can even change a cat's self-image. The following story is an example.

Abdul considered himself a lowly, mangy Egyptian Mau,

until a near-death encounter revealed his regal connec-
tions. He lived in the shadows of the Cairo museum. A guard
had smuggled him in as a starving, flea-ridden stray. He
confesses:

I had no self-esteem. I'd hide out in the storage room or
skulk around the empty museum corridors. The elegant
cat statues of my ancestors only reminded me of how
pedestrian I was.
   The only joy I knew was an odd one. It involved a par-
ticular exhibit in the museum. I derived great pleasure
from rubbing my body against the statues, urns, sacred

vessels, jewelry cases, and furniture from the Ptolemaic
Period—around 51 B.C.

One day, when Abdul was sleeping in a storage room, a
small silver chalice bust toppled off the shelf and fell on his
head. (Today, he believes it was pushed by Her ghost.) He
remembers:

I find myself crossing a river. I'm wrapped in bandages
of white mist, like a mummy.

Out of the darkness, I hear a woman's voice calling:
"Here kitty, kitty—my precious Mau Mau—come kitty,
come kitty, come."

Then suddenly I see her running toward me. Tears of
joy fill her heavily lined almond eyes. Her bangle-laden
arms reach out for me. She grabs me close and kisses my
fur. She is my mistress. My Cleopatra. My Queen.

We're in a fragrant garden, curled up on an ornate
Ptolemaic bed by a lapis blue pool. Cleopatra tries to
anoint my ears with aromatic oil, but I wash it off. She
laughs. Playfully, I bat at the golden asp that hangs in the
middle of her brow. "You haven't changed," she purrs.

"Dearest cat, how can you ever forgive me? I was
such a bad mother, running off to Rome with Caesar, and
then Antony—and leaving you." I tell her all is forgiven,
and we snuggle.

Then she whispers softly that I have to go back. I dig

my claws deep into her pleated tunic and yowl. She comforts me, saying we'll meet again soon.

Suddenly, I'm back in my mangy body on the museum floor. But over time, I sense a change. I hold my head a little higher. I tour the museum in daylight. I delight in occasional pettings. I don't mind being seen.

Deep inside, I know Cleopatra loves me. I'll always be her cat, and she'll always be my Queen.

Cats of the Rich & Famous

A significant number of cats return from their near-death experiences and begin to drop names. Who's who in cat heaven? They'll tell you. It seems everyone has a celebrity connection. These cats claim intimate familiarity with some rich or famous lap. Obviously, there's no proving them wrong. Here are some examples:

Snowball, an overstuffed white Persian living in a Dorchester, England, bakery, says she met Queen Victoria on the astral plane. She says she was the Queen's cat, White Heather, in a previous life. "The Queen's lap was still warm," she said.

A brown tabby named Elvis, who enjoys permanent guest status at the Sands Hotel in Las Vegas, says near-death allowed him to perch on the shoulders of his name-sake. This fur Elvis impurrsonator says they even yowled out some tunes together.

Dusty, a gray-and-white shorthair living around the corner from Ernest Hemingway's house in Key West, Florida, claims to have been Papa's favorite feline and main mews. Dusty says it was hard to locate Ernest on the Other Side—he was buried under a pile of cats.

A Chartreux named Charlotte, who lives in a Paris bookstore, says a near-death experience showed her to have once been Saha, the beloved cat of the great French writer Colette. Charlotte/Saha even claims to be the actual author of Colette's book *La Chatte*.

Edward is a delicate Devon Rex from Blackpool, England, who says his real name is Beppo. He claims that the great British poet Lord Byron gave him that name in a "jolly romantic life." He says he stays in touch by sleeping on Lord Byron's books.

A portly silver British shorthair named Mr. Tibbs says that before he lived in a London butcher shop, he curled up at 10 Downing Street. In fact, he presided over Parlia-

ment! A near-death experience showed him to have been Winston Churchill's cat, Jock, he says.

Many claims have been made, but one truth seems evident: Nothing ends. Names and fur coats may change, but feline souls remain the same.

Astral Fun & Games

I think, therefore I am, whatever I choose to be.
Mau Tzu Pauz

It's no wonder there are so many frequent fliers on the astral plane. It's a journey where cats are never bored. They tell us that in death, there are as many opportunities for adventure as there are in life.

For one thing, on the astral plane you're in your astral fur body, and it doesn't have a care in the world. Your astral fur body doesn't get mats, furballs, tartar on its teeth, or fleas. It's also free of life's little limitations—like time, space, and the need to use the litter box.

Tired of having the same old paws and whiskers? Try being a different color, breed, or species. On the astral plane, you can even change your astral fur body just as fast as you can change your mind. Feel what it's like to be a ladybug, chicken, Chihuahua, cheetah, rosebush, rattlesnake, or snail—separately or all at once!

See yourself in four dimensions, or be invisible. Visit cats on other planets. Travel through time and space. With a little imagination, anything's possible.

Quick-Change Artist

Here's the story of one cat's transformational astral adventure. Puss 'n Boots is a young black-and-white shorthair who admits to watching a lot of TV.

"When I'm not watching it, I'm sleeping on it," she buzzes.

One day, a loose wire zapped Puss right out of her boots. She found herself tuned into a new channel—on the astral plane. She recalls:

Near-death was even more entertaining than watching Feline Feast commercials.

After I breezed through a jumbo Kitty Kibbles tunnel, I watched reruns of my past lives and tracked dead celebrities. Then my guardian angel made a float-on appearance as a special guest. She told me that I was going back but could spend a little more time in my astral fur body, stretching my imagination.

I wanted to see what it was like to be in another creature's paws, so I turned myself into the cheetah from the Adventure Channel. I relished having its power, speed, and spots.

Then I transformed myself into some of my other screen favorites. I was Lassie, Regis, Black Beauty, Toto, Miss Piggy, the Pillsbury Doughboy, Oprah, the Lion King, both Milo *and* Otis, and that prissy Persian cat-food star.

We asked Puss 'n Boots if her astonishing astral journey had made the rest of her life seem dull.

"Not at all," she said. "I learned that dogs and people take direction, puppets are empty-headed, big cats are always hungry, hay tastes crummy, and even Persian superstars get mats. I enjoy being me."

High-Flying Felines

One of the things cats love about near-death is the flexibility of their astral fur bodies. We've heard vivid descriptions of extraordinary high-flying feats. Some cats even claim that out-of-body workouts give them new agility when they return to life.

Typical comments include: "I came back with new courage"; "I can snap my tail like a rubber band"; "Because I no longer fear death, I leap out of tall buildings and fly off trees, knowing I'll land on my feet."

Here's what exercise is like on the astral plane:

- High-speed tail spinning
- Twirling on alternate ears
- Touchdown landings on just one paw
- Twisting your body into a pretzel
- Flapping all four legs like wings
- Soaring catnaps
- Regulating your flying speed with your whiskers
- Short stops on clouds
- Multiple high-speed forward and backward flips
- Tandem flying with a friend
- Twirling on your whiskers
- Undulating your body like a wave.

Appuritions

Disembodied cats have been known to take advantage of their invisibility. They'll scare up old friends, revisit favorite haunts, and often make a nuisance of themselves.

Feline ghosts are known as *appuritions*. Although clairvoyants try to contact them during séances, appuritions are mostly uninvited astral guests who show up when they like.

They can look as real as life or as illusory as thin mist, hazy lights, or a diaphanous veil. They've been known to go through walls, knock over lamps, shred unpaid bills, hide keys, turn over wastebaskets, turn on TVs, and destroy knitting.

Misbehaving appuritions give cats a bad name. Here are some examples.

The Ghost Gourmet

A twenty-pound brown tabby named Gaston says he used his out-of-body state to go on a tour of all his favorite New Orleans kitchens. He was hoping to dine at each.

To his dismay, he discovered that it wasn't possible to eat Oysters Trufant or Crab Bayou with an astral fur body. So Gaston turned himself into an appurition. As a hungry ghost, he made the rounds.

Chef Antoine remembers: "I'm chopping the chicken, and out of nowhere, this brown tabby appears. He tries to grab the food. *Mon dieu!* I almost faint."

After shaking up several famous restaurants and terrifying the guests with floating food and broken crockery, Gaston called it quits. Without a real body, he couldn't satisfy his appetite.

Returning to life, Gaston became a new cat, with a svelte new feline physique.

"Food is so *magnifique*," he says. "Now I eat slowly; I savor every bite."

Show Biz

When appuritions act up, they usually live to regret it. A Balinese grand champion named Angel Face told us that vanity led her to commit an out-of-body crime.

A high fever from a respiratory infection not only knocked her out of her body; it also took her out of the year's most important cat show. As she tells it:

> I couldn't stand the idea of losing my title. I was devastated—being stuck on some cloud, knowing that catnip-abusing Shangri-La of Balimoor was preening in the wings.
>
> I decided to ghost the cat show.
>
> Just as Shangri-La was being shown, I landed on the table. I grabbed the judge's peacock feather in my astral teeth and floated around with it, tormenting my rival.
>
> Shangri-La screeched, clawed the judge in terror, jumped three feet in the air, and flew off the table. Needless to say, she was summarily disqualified.

When Angel Face returned to life, the journey had weakened her body but strengthened her spirit. She quit the cat-show circuit and made her amends. Now, in her job as a national spokescat for Medicat Health Care Benefits, her looks are being put to good use.

The Peeping Tom

We've all heard of Peeping Toms. One Tom did more than peep. He used his near-death experience as an excuse to cuddle up. As Tom tells it:

When I found out I could be invisible, I dropped in on Foxie. But when I looked in the window, I was devastated. Foxie was curled up with that overbearing Burmese stud, Kung Fu.

So I peeped in on that luscious silver vixen, Madame Butterfly, who lives next door. She was sleeping on the sofa—with a moonbeam kissing her silky cheek. I curled up beside her, nestling near her soft, warm fur. She continued to snooze. I rubbed my paw on her head. Nothing. Then I gave her a gentle bite on the back of the neck. Nothing. Madame Butterfly was sound asleep.

I finally began to get the message. The trouble with being invisible is that you are ... *invisible*. Out-of-body peeping has its limitations. It's better to be a Peeping Tom in the fur.

Tom sums it up well. Though astral high jinks may be enjoyable, cats advise you not to mix them up with real life.

No Purring in Purrgatory

Cats who go into the light expecting to find darkness
usually do.

Ancient Tonkinese Teaching

Not all cats paint a rosy picture of the Other Side. The Paw of
Fate directs some cats to visit Purrgatory. Instead of going
up, they go down. It's not a place that cats would choose to
visit. Then how come some cats do?

It's a cosmic cat maxim: Dark thoughts lead you to dark
places. So it's no surprise that accounts of a dark, diabolical
netherworld often come from cats with dark, negative energy.

Prospects for Purrgatory are often cats plagued by guilty
memories of some imagined wrongdoing. Angry, superstitious, and full of fear, these cats see the world as a hostile
place run by a hissing Creator.

For this bunch, Purradise can only follow on the paws of
Purrgatory. But for most, it's a short stopover with a happy
ending. We've seen that even the most insensitive couch

shredders, antisocial hiss-faces, and militant mouse tormentors come back transformed.

A Leaky Basement

The following story comes to us from a Singapura named Dr. Strangelove.

Because of Dr. Strangelove's treacherous scare tactics, every potential companion that his provider brought home was sent packing within a day. He admits:

I wasn't a nice cat. A handsome stud, maybe. But nasty to the core.

I had a near-death experience when I tried to swallow a would-be roommate's pedigree and nearly choked to death.

I left my body and floated down this long, dark staircase. I landed in a damp dungeon of a basement with leaky pipes that dripped on my fur.

I immediately realized I wasn't alone. It was wall-to-wall cats. Cats hissed and snarled and spat and scratched. We vied for territory, trying to avoid the dripping pipes and puddles.

I had no special privileges. In this terrible place, a cat was a cat.

Then, way off in the distance, I heard my loving

provider calling my name. I opened my eyes and was terribly relieved to see I was back.

Mighty Mice

The images of Purrgatory seem to arise from deep within the furry walls of the feline mind. Here's Purrgatory for a cat who chased mice for "sport":

I find myself in a world of giant rodents. I am tiny. They glare at me menacingly with dark, beady eyes. Linking tails, they surround me. I smell cheese on their breath. They force me into a tiny hole from which there is no escape. Monster mice stand guard. I hear the sound of gnawing. The rodent population is celebrating my capture with huge wedges of Norwegian Jarlsberg and giant rounds of ripe Brie.

A Rotten Life Revisited

For Boots, Purrgatory was a visit to a miserable medieval past life where cats were hated, hunted, and forever on the run. Her near-death experience took place during kitten birth. Boots recalls:

Suddenly, I'm back in the Dark Ages. Men in robes race after me. I'm running over wet cobblestones. People rush out of doorways, trying to catch me. They have baskets and nets. I'm terrified. I know that if they catch me, it's the end.

I float back into my body. One of my beautiful new kittens mews. I realize I'm not dead.

After this frightening trip down memory lane, Boots tried past-life regression therapy. She scratched around in her past and found she carried guilt from a former life in medieval Spain.

During this life, she says, all the cats in her family were captured and burned at the stake. Boots lived, hidden in the cellar. But as the lone feline survivor of those terrible times, she always felt guilty.

The past-life regression sessions helped Boots finally see her own worth. As she puts it, "Now I understand the meaning of my lives. They prepared me to be a better mother. The love and protection that I was given is something I can return."

Armed Sofa Warfare

Some cats who visit Purrgatory come back with a new respect for everything on the planet. Even things they treated "like furniture" are seen in a new light. Take the following ac-

count. Chang Mai, an elegant chocolate point Siamese, always thought a couch had three purposes: bed, nail file, and trampoline. When it got old and shredded, you just bought a new one.

As Chang Mai tore its fat chintz arm to tatters, the couch never complained. But during a near-death experience, Chang Mai discovered the sofa had something to say.

I'm floating out in space, and all of a sudden—out of nowhere—an army of sofas surrounds me!

I'm trapped in the middle of them. They fire at me—furiously hurling their bolsters, cushions, pillows, and foam-rubber seats.

Angry love seats flip on their sides and sweep me along like angry brooms. Sectional sofas fly at me in strategic formation. They spit out their stuffing, cotton batting, Fiberglas, and foam.

I try to run for cover, but there's no sofa I can hide under. "Stop! Stop!" I cry, promising never to scratch the furniture again.

As chilling as Purrgatory may sound, cats who've gone there and come back consider their visit a valuable learning experience. We've also found that subsequent near-death experiences lead to the light.

Socrates, a philosophical fourteen-year-old tiger tabby with fifteen near-death experiences under his collar, sums it up best when he says, "You learn to roll with death—as you do with life. You find things to purr about. I don't let life or death get me too carried away."

Nine Lives Review

Looking back, the wise cat sees exactly where his tail
has been.

Catfuscious

Imagine curling up in front of a movie in which you star—which costars everyone you've ever met, eyeballed, or casually brushed tails with—that has a script from your own nine lives.

Imagine watching intimate scenes from these past lives in a high-speed hologram that surrounds you with images, sounds, and smells.

As big numbers of your past lives flash by, imagine witnessing all your nasty transgressions, random acts of kindness, destructive snits, and sweet, cuddly moments—all over again.

Imagine refeeling all your old feelings, along with everyone else's. Imagine knowing what everyone else was thinking at the time.

Imagine being the sole judge of everything you've ever thought, felt, or done. And learning from it all.

The Nine Lives Review is all this. And more.

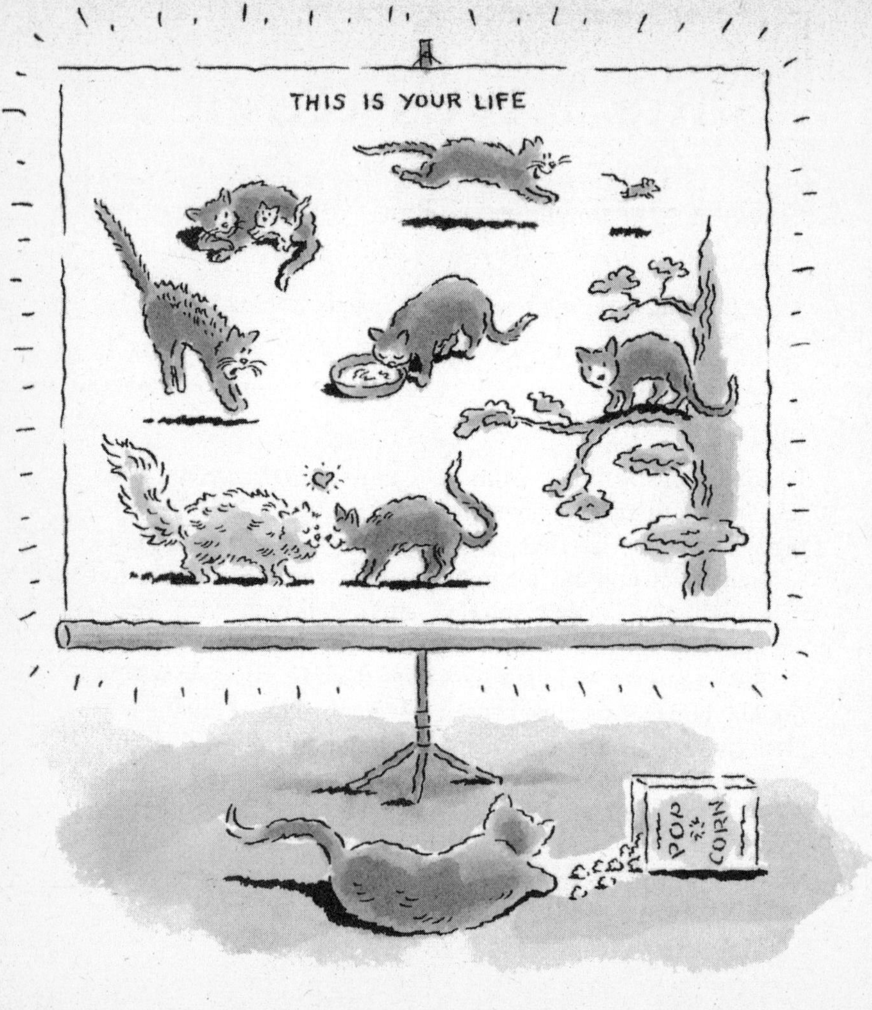
THIS IS YOUR LIFE
POP CORN

Why Was I So Aloof?

For a glamorous but remote white Angora named Powder Puff, the Nine Lives Review offered some valuable lessons in love.

Powder Puff says the wild struggle she put up in a bubble bath is what caused her near-death. Before she knew it, she was floating up over the tub, looking down at the wet mess of fur that was her. Here's what happened next:

"No more baths," I think to myself as I float up toward the Furry Gates.

Then all at once I see my guardian angel. She doesn't look happy. Both ears are back. And her emerald eyes glow.

"Not so fast, Powder Puff," she hisses. "After your Nine Lives Review, you're going back."

"Can't I just float up to the Furry Gates?" I beg. By her flipping tail, I can see she means "no way."

Then all at once I'm in my Nine Lives Review.

Suddenly I'm in ancient Siam, where I see myself as a vain Siamese temple cat. I watch as a humble man enters the temple to bring me a dish of milk and worship at my paws. I sneer and walk away.

Next, I'm in Germany during the Middle Ages. I'm lying at the foot of an enormous fireplace. There's a Rottweiler by my side. Ludwig rolls over, trying to be friendly and eager to play. I give him a vicious swipe on the nose, snarl, hiss, and walk away.

Next I find myself in a suburb of Sydney, Australia. My family is putting up posters that say "Lost Cat" because I've run away. The children are crying. The parents tell them I'll return—but in fact I never do.

"Seen enough, Powder Puff?" my guardian angel asks.

"Yes! Yes!" I yowl.

With that, I'm back in the tub. Only seconds have passed. I leap into my person's arms. I purr loudly in her ear. I nuzzle her with my nose. I rub against her cheek with my bubble-covered fur.

The next time I review a past life, I want to watch scenes that are filled with love.

A Real Hooligan

After spending eight lives on the edge, a feisty Irish tabby named Hooligan finally got kicked Upstairs.

During Hooligan's Nine Lives Review, he got to see the "ripple effect" of his reckless shenanigans. As he tells it:

I didn't know what hit me. But when I floated out of my body, I got a better perspective.

I saw it was Paddy, from the saloon. I ran right into him as I was dodging traffic. Thought I was dead.

As I'm floating up, I meet my guardian angel—the same fuzzy bloke who keeps saving my life.

He takes me through the tunnel. I figure we're going to meet the Main Cat in charge.

"Not this time, Hooligan," he says. "You're going back after a Nine Lives Review."

All of a sudden I see myself living in a fancy castle, gaily swinging from a crystal chandelier. When the butler discovers me, I spring to the mantel, knock over a Ming vase, and quickly disappear. Suddenly, I feel what it's like to be the butler and take the blame. I feel awful.

In another life, I'm in Copenhagen, and it's pouring rain. I see myself dart across a street. A bicycle tries to avoid me and crashes into a fence. Suddenly, I feel what it's like to be the angry driver on a bashed-up bike. I feel terrible.

Next, I find myself in the back alleys of Dublin. For weeks I've been prowling the streets, catting around. Suddenly, I feel what it's like to be my beloved person, missing my whiskers and desperately wishing I'd crawl in the door.

My guardian angel watches my anguish with obvious delight. "Hooligan, do you think you could try being a decent cat in your one remaining life?" he asks. I promise that I will.

With that, I'm back in my disheveled fur coat, lying on the bar with Paddy petting my face. I give him a warm lick on the hand. But that was just a taste of the love that was to come.

No More Clean Plates

The Nine Lives Review has also shown itself to be a valuable therapeutic tool. Past lives are often the cause of present behaviors.

Dolly is a good example. Before her near-death experience from choking on a Yummy Bit, Dolly, a shapely white short-hair, tells us she lived to eat. "Kitty Bites and Yummy Bits were my downfall," she says.

During her Nine Lives Review, Dolly saw that in several previous lives, she'd been a homeless, hungry stray.

"I had a poor, starving cat inside of me who was meowing to be fed," she told us.

Dolly says that by gaining new self-understanding she's lost the need to clean her plate.

A Scent of My Own

By revisiting his former lives, an immaculate seal point Siamese named Sherwood was able to find out why he was forever washing his fur. As he tells it:

During the Nine Lives Review, I got a whiff of my past.

During a life in Catlantis, I was the patchouli-scented pet of an aromatherapist.

As the cat of an affectionate French countess who smothered me in perfumed kisses, I smelled like *L'Amour dangereux.*

During my last life with a Los Angeles hairdresser, I smelled like shampoo.

By the end of my Nine Lives Review, I understood. All I ever wanted was a scent of my own.

My Forever Person

For one cat, the Nine Lives Review revealed the truth about a long and treasured relationship.

Miss Merrywhite and Mabel were inseparable. And when Mabel, a twenty-year-old brown tabby, left her body during a short illness, she refused to leave Miss Merrywhite's side. Miss Merrywhite was also near death. So she floated by her bed.

"If my guardian angel hadn't grabbed me by the paw and

dragged me to the Other Side, I never would have left," Mabel tells us.

But she's glad she made the journey. During her Nine Lives Review, Mabel got to see how she and Miss Merrywhite had been together since the beginning of time. She says:

> Of course, I wasn't always a cat called Mabel, and she wasn't always a lady called Miss Merrywhite. We were other sexes, had other names, and even lived on other planets. But I was relieved to see that we were always good friends.
>
> For example, in one life I was a fierce African lion and Miss Merrywhite was a brave hunter named Kimbo. Because we recognized each other, neither of us was harmed.
>
> In another life, Miss Merrywhite was a pampered Chinese princess and I was her cherished Birman cat.
>
> During Miss Merrywhite's life as a struggling Pilgrim farmer in New England, I helped her keep rats out of the barn.
>
> Once, Miss Merrywhite was reincarnated as a woman who was allergic to cats. I knew she was aching to pet me. I lived right next door.

When Mabel returned to Miss Merrywhite, her heart was filled with joy. She knew that even though they might part, they'd never say good-bye.

The Nine Lives Review is full of small lessons that help cats evaluate their spiritual progress and chart their future course.

More Lives to Live: The Return

> The path from life to death is not scent-marked.
>
> Upurrandshed Sutra

It's no wonder the veil between life and death is covered with fur. There's a lot of cat traffic. With nine lives to live, the odds of a cat having a near-death experience are exceptionally high: By the top of the ninth life, 95 percent of cats have had at least one near-death experience, while 80 percent report having had two or more.

We're told that the Other Side is so filled with love, beauty, and fine opportunities for rest, growth, and stimulating adventure that most cats put up some resistance when it's time to go.

What's the return trip like? Some cats say they're suddenly "sucked in" or "lapped up" by their earthbound forms. Some report popping back in through the space between their ears. One traveler to the Darkside claims he reentered through his tail. Many say it's like being awakened suddenly from a catnap.

Once back, acceptance quickly sets in, and any fear of death is forever gone.

I Saw Purradise

Inga is a Norwegian Forest cat who lives in a small Oslo apartment. She says her life was rather mundane until a mysterious fever caused a near-death experience she'll never forget.

In the distance, I saw Purradise. A glorious carpet-covered city. There were Kitty Kastles and Kitty Kondos upholstered in every conceivable color and texture. Tufted turrets. Nubby porches. Fuzzy terraces. And all over the city, inviting, cozy spots for cats to perch.

I raced toward the city with a pounding heart. I could see the Gates of Purradise right ahead. All I had to do was climb the quilted fence.

Then, out of nowhere, a radiant silver Persian angel appeared. Right in my path. Sparkles danced off her whiskers. White diamonds shone on her fur. And she was in my way.

"Inga, you're going back to Oslo," she purred sweetly.

"No! No!" I yowled. "Please let me visit Purradise!"

Then I grabbed the fence with both paws and dug in with my claws.

"Inga, if you die now, you'll be missing a wonderful life. Let me show you."

Then all at once I was in my Oslo apartment—watching a scene from my future life.

I saw my bushy-tailed future mate, stretched out on the floor, taking me in with his sensuous green eyes. And there was I, proud and purring, with my new litter of kittens.

"You don't want to miss this," the angel whispered. And I didn't. "I guess Purradise can wait," I said. And it has.

Cats Try Every Trick

For many felines, the desire to remain on the Other Side is so powerful they'll try every trick. A desperate white Turkish Van dug a deep hole in a cloud, dove in, and refused to come out.

A streetwise tom tried to bribe his guardian angel with tins of fancy imported fish, while a smooth-talking Chartreux sashayed around, shedding his Gallic charm.

One cat we spoke with even had some temporary success. A clever Sphinx projected himself to another galaxy, blended in with the feline-noids, and extended his stay.

Transfurmations

To be a work of art is the reason for my existence.
Birman Grand Champion Maximilian of Silkypaws
(Before his near-death experience)

For each cat who walks the earth, there is an earthly
purpose—having to do with love.
Birman Grand Champion Maximilian of Silkypaws
(After his near-death experience)

Our research on feline near-death has made one thing perfectly clear: The experience is always transfurmational. The lessons that cats bring back from the Other Side invariably alter the course of their remaining lives.

There are as many kinds of transfurmations as there are cats, but they're all for the good. Sometimes a cat who has had a near-death experience becomes more cuddly and caring. Sometimes there's a behavioral shift, from selfish to self-sacrificing. Sometimes a cat's complete purrsona undergoes a radical change.

Cats who've committed sins against the fur find new respect

for their bodies. Catnip abusers choose abstinent lives. Unrelenting bullies suddenly roll on their backs. Runaways stay at home. Homebodies go out and explore. The transfurmations are often profound. Even the most hostile couch shredders will give up the scratch, transforming free-floating anger into meaningful love.

Besides witnessing extraordinary behavioral changes, we've also found evidence of amazing physical, psychic, and spiritual changes. Many cats report increased sensitivity to light and sound, and can see a noticeable force field around their fur that gives them an otherworldly glow.

Some cats become electromagnetic marvels, with heightened paranormal powers. Some discover they have miraculous healing powers right in their paws.

And a few, like author Fluffy Beadie, find themselves meowing their message to enraptured audiences around the world.

Most cats return with a "mission" of some sort. Usually, it's the desire to create a world with more love. More love between animals and animals, animals and people, people and people, all life on the planet and the planet itself.

Without exception, every cat we talked to said in near-death they'd learned the meaning of life. And the meaning is love.

Street Cat Turned Social Worker

Bojangles is a stocky, shorthaired gray tom who's missing part of an ear. This itinerant street fighter has known a mean

life in the alleys. Always a loner. Existing by his wits. Never trusting life.

"I'd bite the hand that fed me," he says.

A near-death experience changed his outlook on everything. He learned you've got to love yourself first. "While some nice folks who had rescued me from the streets were nursing me back to health, I floated around heaven and learned that every cat deserves deep adoration, decent food, and respect. My mission was to come back and spread the news.

"Now I work the back alleys, helping strays like myself. Recently, I started an outreach center called 'Hip Cats.' We focus on feline self-esteem. Down-and-out street cats learn how to clean up their coats, locate generous restaurants, and sniff out good homes."

Not Business as Usual

Before the watermelon landed on her head, Beansprout had no sense of her charisma, sales ability, or charm. This beige-and-white shorthair looked at the world through sleepy and cynical golden eyes.

"I never liked my job at the greengrocer," she tells us. "I'd spend my days sleeping in the empty apple crates. If I was awake, I'd rip the lettuce to shreds for fun. I hissed at anyone who came near the catnip. I'd nip at people's ankles. My only contribution to Wang's Vegetable Stand was steadily shrinking sales.

"In near-death, I was shown the spiritual mission in my job. I learned the value of simply giving and receiving love. Now every day, I greet customers at the door with a soft purr and a friendly ankle rub. I help with advertising and window display by lying beside the cut flowers in the front of the store. I meow hello to every customer and always answer to my name. Business is booming."

Aristocrat Turned Animal Activist

Anna Karenina is a three-time grand champion Russian Blue of royal lineage. Before her near-asphyxiation from noxious paint fumes, her days were spent doing her nails and reading *CATS Magazine.*

Anna, who was known as "the silent queen of the cat-show circuit," knew how to woo the judges with a whisker. Beyond that, she says, "I was totally vapid. All I had between my ears was fur."

On the Other Side, Anna was shown how to put her beauty and breeding to work on behalf of felines less fortunate than herself. Today she's an outspoken animal rights activist and a crusader for feline equality.

"Someday Doris Day, Paul and Linda McCartney, and Brigitte Bardot may ask me to sit on their laps," she jokes.

Anna is also starting a nationwide chain of luxuriously appointed animal shelters, which she says she'll fund herself.

"I want Baltic blue wall-to-wall carpeting everywhere—even on the walls!" she purrs.

Coffeehouse Clairvoyant

The transfurmation of a young striped shorthair named Catpuccino provided us with a glowing example of the heightened psychic powers that many cats display after near-death.

"Before I choked on that Indonesian coffee bean, I was nothing but an idle coffeehouse cat," Catpuccino confesses.

"I was totally self-obsessed. I reserved the best window banquette for my naps. I placed myself between people and their reading matter. I even delighted in pouncing on intense chess games right near the end."

After he recovered from near-death, the first thing that Catpuccino noticed was his fur. It glowed.

"Everyone in the coffeehouse could see it. There was a bright, bluish light all around my coat. And when people petted me, they said they got a nice buzz."

Soon after that, Catpuccino discovered he had an astonishing new range of clairvoyant powers:

I was so supercharged that clocks would stop, the TV would levitate, lights would blink, and cups would fly off the tables when I'd pass by. I made static on the stereo and changed songs on the antique jukebox. It was wild.

Then I started giving customers information they were meant to read. I'd locate passages in newspapers or magazines and sit on them, or push appropriate books off the shelves with my paw.

I began to read minds, forecast the weather, and do healings—by laying my paws on people or just by simply resting on their laps.

Catpuccino tells us he loves his present life because, for the first time, he feels useful.

"I'm only a fur vehicle," he says.

Nursing-Home Volunteer

Princess Di admits that before her near-death experience she was an overly pampered Persian whose life focused on the maintenance of her luxurious apricot fur coat.

"I was a very shallow cat," she says. "All I ever did was sleep and eat and allow myself to be combed."

When a food allergy carried Princess Di to death's door, she peeked in and saw the light.

When she came back, she had a mission. Princess Di became a nursing-home volunteer.

Today Princess Di is the wonder cat of the health-care world. She's a natural feline healer who helps to lower blood pressure, cure depression, speed recoveries, bring smiles to everyone she sits on, and promote longer, happier lives.

"They call me 'The Furry Fountain of Youth,' " she purrs, fluffing up with a new kind of pride.

Feline Wisdom

For some final insights on the transfurmational power of the near-death experience, we talked to an authority on feline spirituality. A cat named Quincy.

Quincy is a charismatic silver tabby who says he gets his wisdom from forty-two near-death experiences and twenty years of good living.

He says that after each brush with death, he feels "more spiritually well groomed. I feel shinier, happier, and more beautiful—inside and out," he purrs.

"When you scratch on death's door," he says, "and it opens, you see there's a lot going on inside. It's certainly not death."

 *The Cat Credo*

1. Be kind to everyone. One of them might be your past or future mother.
2. Never bite a hand that feeds you.
3. Try walking ten miles in someone else's paws.
4. If you claw your way to the top, you still have to climb down.
5. Remember: Fleas have feelings too.
6. Your fur coat is on loan. Treat it with respect.
7. Don't do anything you wouldn't want to watch on a big screen.
8. Remember that in the universe, you're simply a furball of frozen light.
9. A purr is your gift to the world. Use it well.

The Burmese Book of the Dead

Cats who go around come around.
Catskrit Proverb

No discussion of near-death would be complete without mentioning one of the most sacred of all feline manuscripts, *The Burmese Book of the Dead*.

The Burmese Book of the Dead tells cats how to die, what to do while dead, how to avoid rebirth, or, failing that, how to do everything possible to assure that the next set of nine lives will be good.

The original text was clawed in Catskrit by an enlightened feline named Purrdmasambhava in the eighth century. Although he buried the book behind his monastery, it was quickly discovered by a temple cat going about his business, digging in the dirt.

The original manuscript was in ragged condition—shredded in spots where the cat scratching had caused large rips. Nonetheless, some fragments survive, here roughly translated from the original Catskrit meowed at the time.

O nobly born [name of cat],
the time hath now come for thee to take to the pathway of light between thy ears.
Thou art about to experience the Purrdo State,
wherein all things are spotless and pure, like a newly cleansed coat.
Pray thusly:
May I be led by the Pure Radiance of Discriminating Wisdom.
May the Purring Luminous White Mother guard my tail.
May the Purring Luminous Silver Mother guard my back.
May I be placed within the Pure Realms of Purradise.

Even if you've just been hit by a rickshaw, Purrdmasambhava suggests exiting from your body in as spiritual a frame of mind as possible. If you're angry at the rickshaw driver or mad because the squirrel made it across the street and you didn't, you'll have negative thoughts, which can contribute to a rotten rebirth. He recommends that you meditate on your favorite feline deity and let go.

To deal with all the unusual manifestations on the astral plane, Purrdmasambhava suggests:

O nobly born, perk up thine ears. Notice that thou hast a body of light—thine earth body having been cast off like a cat costume once worn in a play.

O nobly born, since thou hast not a fur body, whatever may come—sounds, lights, nasty appuritions—know that they are unable to harm thee. Know them to be from thine own feline thoughts.

O nobly born feline—notice that thou hast the power to pass through mountains, float over trees, change form, or fly like the birds on the wing.

O nobly born feline, thou wilt see creatures on the earth plane and they will not see you. Thou wilt not see thy pawprints on the ground. Seeing thy food vessel gone, thou thinkest, "I am dead!" Do not be attached.

O nobly born feline, when thou seest the Great Judger, deep brown in color, with three heads, twelve ears, fifteen paws, ninety-seven claws, five tails, growling, hissing, snarling, fur emitting flames of radiance, and a tablet bearing to thy sins, fear it not. Know it to be thy self. Thou art thine own judger.

Wishing cats a fortunate rebirth, Purrdmasambhava closes with these words:

O nobly born feline, driven by longing for the earth scents, thou wilt pass back through the Void, entering into thy mother, who will deliver thee to life. Walk with thy tail held high. Choose the path of Radiant Light.

NOTE: It's said that the original manuscript was reburied near a Pet Emporium in the suburbs of Rangoon. Recently, a Burmese local made claw contact with what he thought was part of the manuscript. It turned out to be shredded fast-food menus. At last report, cats are still digging.

A Near-Death Questionnaire

Have you had a near-death experience? Take this test. Check all the answers that apply.

1) The last time I was out of my body was . . .
   a. While mating.
   b. While being altered.
   c. While having kittens.
   d. When they brought home the new baby.
   e. After almost dying.

2) I knew I was dead because . . .
   a. I was invisible to mice.
   b. My fleas and mats were gone.
   c. My cat food tasted like air.
   d. My astral fur body had an astral scent.
   e. I didn't have to use the litter box.

3) Floating over my dead body, I thought . . .
    a. I can't believe it's me!
    b. Poor thing.
    c. Good riddance.
    d. Nice cat suit.
    e. I thought I was better-looking.

4) My Tunnel experience could be best described as being . . .
    a. In a long, dark passageway.
    b. Inside a paper bag.
    c. Inside a shopping bag.
    d. In a dark closet.
    e. Under the covers.

5) I was lured into the Tunnel by . . .
    a. Cat angels.
    b. Whiskered Light Beings.
    c. Old pals who've passed on.
    d. Enticing sounds and smells.
    e. An invisible force.

6) My experience of the Light can be compared to . . .
    a. Basking under a lamp.
    b. Sitting on a pile of warm laundry.
    c. Lying as close to the space heater as I can get.
    d. The ultimate sunbathing spot on a sunny day.
    e. Being cuddled, stroked, petted, and loved.

7) In the afterlife, I found I could communicate with . . .
   a. Animal life.
   b. Human life.
   c. Vegetable and mineral life.
   d. Anyone and anything that came into my mind.

8) In my Nine Lives Review I learned . . .
   a. Love your fellow creatures as yourself.
   b. Share your catnip.
   c. Show dogs more respect.
   d. Insects aren't toys.
   e. People need you more than you need them.

9) The Creator I met in my near-death experience . . .
   a. Had whiskers.
   b. Had paws of pure light.
   c. Had no scent.
   d. Knew what I'd done to that sofa.

10) As a result of my near-death experience I notice:
   a. A strange glow around my fur.
   b. That animals and children try to snuggle with me.
   c. That electrical appliances go haywire in my presence.
   d. When people pet me they get buzzed.

11) My new psychic abilities include . . .
     a. My paws have healing power.
     b. I know when I'm about to be fed.
     c. I cause cat food to fly off the shelf.
     d. I see and read cat auras.

12) Some highlights of near-death included . . .
     a. Being heated in the Warming Room.
     b. Heavenly sounds and smells.
     c. Cruising my old haunts.
     d. Lap hopping.
     e. Meeting my Maker.

13) After my near-death experience, I became . . .
     a. Incredibly cuddly, snuggly, and sweet.
     b. A wild daredevil who lives on the edge.
     c. A fearless feline who stands up to bullies.
     d. A feline Pied Piper who leads home needy strays.
     e. A celebrity everyone wants to sniff.

14) The reason for my return to life was . . .
     a. My "other half" was waiting for me.
     b. My people needed me.
     c. I had five kittens to raise.
     d. I wanted to scratch out a book about my experience.
     e. My nine lives weren't up.

15) The purpose of life is . . .
    a. Eating.
    b. Sleeping.
    c. Chasing things that move.
    d. Sharing your purr.

Final Mewsings

Catnaps above, catnaps below.
Catskrit Proverb

Through their experiences on the Other Side, cats have begun to shred the thin veil between life and death. Outmoded beliefs and meaningless fears are being ripped away.

Cats who've been exposed to the other reality can't shut it out. Their purrsonalities, living patterns, and spiritual beliefs are forever altered.

Near-death brings cats closer to the meaning of life. They lose their fear of death and find new zest in living. They learn they are love.

Out of all the many cats who've had near-death experiences, only a comparative pawful have come forth to provide detailed reports. For fear of being hissed at, many cats are still afraid to go public. But we believe this is changing.

As the incredible psychic abilities of felines become more widely accepted, cat testimonies about the Hereafter will

surely carry special weight. Morever, the ancient Eastern feline belief in reincatnation (multiple nine lives) is now being validated by near-death.

The profoundly heightened psychic powers of cats who've come back also suggest that the near-death experience may have far-reaching implications for feline evolution. These cats may represent the next stage: high-frequency felines poised to Ascend.

We're seeing that physical reality is only one corner of the dish. For every sofa down here, there's one that's equally soft up there.

As cats discover their own true natures, they discover their lives' special purrpose. And so many, like a golden tabby named Sunflower, find it's a simple expression of love.

I never would have believed that anything as basic to my being, and as effortless as my purr, could be the key to my own spiritual path.

But on the Other Side, a Light Being reminded me that my purr has the power to heal and create happiness.

He said that I had an exceptionally powerful purr and my mission was to let the world hear it.

By looking at these experiences, we see the feline as a continuing spiritual being, operating in a physical fur vehicle, or an astral fur vehicle, depending on the road.

For cats who've experienced near-death, immortality is no longer just a possibility—it's a fact. When your nine lives are up, you can look forward to more.